DEBATE

THE

COLLAPSE

OF

COMMUNICATION

Where debate creates noise,
discussion restores clarity

Dedication

For those who have ever felt unheard,

misunderstood,

or lost inside a conversation that never touched what was real.

For the ones who kept reaching for clarity

even when the world rewarded noise.

For every mind that longed to be seen

without having to fight,

perform,

or defend itself.

This book is for you.

May you find the courage to slow down,

the strength to return to reality,

and the quiet confidence to speak from truth

rather than fear.

And may your conversations —

with others,

with the world,

and with yourself —

become places where understanding can finally live.

PART I: BOOK THESIS

CHAPTER 1 — THE LINE WE CROSS

Debate has become the dominant form of communication in our world.

It fills classrooms, parliaments, pulpits, newsrooms, and social media feeds.

It is celebrated as a sign of intelligence, confidence, and strength.

Yet for all its visibility, debate rarely produces clarity.

It produces noise.

Debate rewards performance over understanding, victory over truth, and identity over honesty.

It is a structure built to win, not to learn.

Discussion is different.

Discussion is cooperative rather than adversarial.

It seeks understanding rather than dominance.

It invites reflection rather than reaction.

Where debate produces noise, discussion produces understanding.

And understanding is the only path to truth.

This book examines the architecture of debate, the confusion it generates, and the clarity that only discussion can restore.

It is not an attack on people, but an examination of a method.

A method that fails.

And a method we can replace.

CHAPTER 2 — DEBATE AS THE DEFAULT

Debate is not something we consciously choose.
It is the method we inherit.

We grow up surrounded by it.
We watch it in classrooms, where students compete
for the "right" answer.
We see it in politics, where candidates are rewarded
for attacking rather than understanding.
We hear it in media, where conflict is more
profitable than clarity.

Debate becomes the default not because it
works, but because it is everywhere.

It is the structure we absorb without noticing.
A method we imitate before we ever question it.
A habit that feels natural simply because it is
familiar.

But familiarity is not the same as truth.
And repetition is not the same as understanding.

Debate persists because it is simple to perform.
It requires no listening, no reflection, no humility.
Only speed, confidence, and the ability to defend a
position — even when that position is weak.

In a world that rewards certainty, debate thrives.
In a world that fears silence, debate fills the space.
In a world that values victory, debate becomes the
only language we know.

But the fact that debate is the default does not
mean it is the best.
It only means we have not yet learned another way.

CHAPTER 3 — WHY THIS BOOK EXISTS

This book exists because something essential has been lost.

We live in a world overflowing with information yet starving for understanding.
We argue more than ever, but we understand each other less.
We speak louder, faster, and with more certainty, but our clarity has not improved.
If anything, it has collapsed.

Debate has become the dominant structure of communication, not because it leads to truth, but because it is familiar, dramatic, and easy to perform.
It rewards confidence over accuracy, speed over reflection, and victory over wisdom.

But human beings do not grow through victory. We grow through understanding.

This book exists to restore that possibility.

It exists to show that debate is not the only way — and not the best way — to think, speak, or discover truth.
It exists to reveal the architecture of noise, the mechanisms that create confusion, and the reasons we keep returning to a method that fails us.

Most importantly, this book exists to offer an alternative.
A way of speaking that does not require winners and losers.
A way of listening that does not demand defensiveness.
A way of thinking that does not collapse under pressure.

A way of being human that is not built on noise.

This book is not a call to silence.

It is a call to clarity.

A call to understanding.

A call to truth.

And truth is worth more than victory.

PART II — THE PROBLEM

CHAPTER 4 — THE RISE OF NOISE

Noise does not appear suddenly.
It grows slowly, quietly, and almost invisibly.

It begins when speed becomes more important than accuracy.
When confidence becomes more valuable than humility.
When speaking becomes more rewarded than listening.

Noise rises when communication becomes a performance.
When the goal shifts from understanding to appearing right.
When the structure of conversation rewards reaction instead of reflection.

We live in a world that amplifies noise because noise is easy to produce.
It requires no discipline, no patience, no depth.
Only volume.

Noise spreads because it feels like activity.
It creates the illusion of engagement, the illusion of progress, the illusion of intelligence.
But noise is not progress.
Noise is the collapse of clarity disguised as communication.

The rise of noise is not a cultural accident.
It is the predictable result of a world that values speed over truth, certainty over curiosity, and performance over understanding.

Noise grows wherever debate becomes the default.
And debate has become the default everywhere.

CHAPTER 5 — THE COLLAPSE OF CLARITY

Clarity does not disappear all at once.
It erodes.

It erodes when conversations become competitions.
It erodes when listening becomes optional.
It erodes when the goal shifts from understanding to defending a position.

Clarity collapses the moment we stop asking,
"What is true?"
and begin asking,
"How do I win?"

When debate becomes the default, clarity becomes the casualty.
Because debate does not reward truth — it rewards survival.
It rewards the ability to defend a claim, not the willingness to examine it.
It rewards the appearance of certainty, not the pursuit of understanding.

Clarity collapses when we treat communication as a battlefield.
When every question becomes a trap.
When every statement becomes a weapon.
When every silence becomes a weakness.

In this environment, truth becomes secondary.
Accuracy becomes negotiable.
Understanding becomes irrelevant.

What matters is the performance.

The collapse of clarity is not a failure of intelligence.
It is a failure of structure.

A structure that encourages noise, accelerates reaction, and punishes reflection.

Clarity cannot survive in a system designed for victory.

It can only survive in a system designed for understanding.

And that system is not debate.

CHAPTER 6 — THE ILLUSION OF "WINNING"

Winning feels satisfying.

It gives us a momentary sense of control, certainty, and superiority.

But in communication, "winning" is almost always an illusion.

You can win an argument without being right.

You can win a debate without understanding anything.

You can win a point while losing the truth.

Winning in debate is not a measure of accuracy. It is a measure of performance.

The person who speaks faster, louder, or with more confidence often appears to win — even when their reasoning is weak.

The person who hesitates, reflects, or considers nuance often appears to lose — even when their understanding is deeper.

Debate creates a world where appearance replaces substance.

Where certainty replaces curiosity.

Where victory replaces truth.

The illusion of winning is powerful because it rewards the ego.

It gives us a sense of identity, a sense of competence, a sense of superiority.

But these feelings are temporary, fragile, and disconnected from reality.

Winning does not make us wiser.

It does not make us clearer.

It does not bring us closer to truth.

It only reinforces the structure that keeps us confused.

The illusion of winning is one of the main reasons debate persists.
It feels good.
It feels powerful.
It feels like progress.

But it is not progress.
It is the performance of progress.

And as long as we chase the feeling of winning, we will never discover the clarity that only understanding can provide.

CHAPTER 7 — THE EGO ENGINE

Beneath every debate, beneath every argument, beneath every performance of certainty, there is an engine running quietly in the background.

The ego.

The ego is not evil.

It is simply loud.

It wants to be right.

It wants to be seen.

It wants to be safe.

Debate gives the ego everything it craves.

A position to defend.

An opponent to defeat.

An audience to impress.

In debate, the ego feels alive.

It feels powerful.

It feels necessary.

But the ego is not interested in truth.

It is interested in survival.

It is interested in identity.

It is interested in protecting the story it tells about itself.

The ego engine turns every conversation into a battlefield.

Every question becomes a threat.

Every correction becomes an attack.

Every moment of uncertainty becomes a danger.

When the ego is driving, understanding becomes impossible.

Because understanding requires vulnerability.

It requires the willingness to be wrong.

It requires the courage to let go of a position long enough to see clearly.

The ego cannot allow that.
It would rather win than understand.
It would rather defend than discover.
It would rather protect its identity than pursue the truth.

This is why debate feels natural.
Not because it is wise, but because it is familiar to the ego.
It mirrors the ego's instincts: defend, attack, survive.

But a method built on ego cannot lead to clarity.
It can only lead to noise.

To understand anything deeply, the ego must step aside.
And debate does not allow that.

CHAPTER 8 — THE STRUCTURE THAT FAILS

Debate is not broken because people are unskilled.

It is broken because the structure itself cannot produce understanding.

A structure built for victory cannot reveal truth. A structure built for performance cannot create clarity.

A structure built on ego cannot generate wisdom.

Debate fails because it is designed to fail.

It divides people into sides before the conversation even begins.

It forces positions before understanding.

It rewards certainty before reflection.

It punishes vulnerability, nuance, and curiosity — the very qualities required for real insight.

Debate turns communication into a contest. And contests require winners and losers.

Once the structure demands a winner, the purpose of the conversation changes.

It is no longer about discovering what is true.

It is about defending what is familiar.

The structure of debate encourages:

- reaction instead of reflection
- defense instead of discovery
- identity instead of honesty
- noise instead of clarity

Even when both people are intelligent, sincere, and well-intentioned, the structure still fails them.

Because the structure is stronger than the individuals inside it.

A failing structure cannot produce a successful outcome.

No amount of skill can compensate for a method that is fundamentally misaligned with truth.

Debate is not the problem because people misuse it.

Debate is the problem because people use it exactly as designed.

And it still fails.

To move toward understanding, we must move beyond the structure that cannot deliver it.

PART III: THE ALTERNATIVE

Debate is not the only way to communicate.
It is simply the most familiar.

There is another structure — quieter, slower, and far more powerful.
A structure built not on victory, but on understanding.
Not on performance, but on clarity.
Not on ego, but on truth.

Part III introduces that structure.

It reveals the method that debate hides.
The method that restores clarity where noise once dominated.
The method that allows two people to think together rather than fight alone.

This part is not about techniques or tricks.
It is about a different way of being in conversation.
A different posture of mind.
A different architecture of truth.

Where debate divides, this method unites.
Where debate accelerates, this method slows.
Where debate demands certainty, this method invites discovery.

This is the alternative.

CHAPTER 9 — THE TURN TOWARD UNDERSTANDING

Understanding does not happen by accident.
It begins with a turn.

A turn away from performance.
A turn away from certainty.
A turn away from the instinct to defend, react, and win.

Understanding begins the moment we choose to step out of the structure that fails us.

This turn is subtle.
It does not require a speech, a declaration, or a dramatic gesture.
It requires only a shift in posture — a willingness to see rather than to win, to listen rather than to defend, to discover rather than to perform.

The turn toward understanding is not a technique.
It is a decision.
A decision to value truth over victory.
A decision to value clarity over comfort.
A decision to value reality over identity.

This turn changes everything.
It changes the pace of the conversation.
It changes the tone.
It changes the purpose.

When we turn toward understanding, we stop preparing our next argument and start paying attention.
We stop defending our position and start examining it.
We stop trying to win and start trying to see.

This turn is the doorway to a different kind of communication — one that is not built on ego, noise, or performance.

It is the doorway to clarity.

And clarity begins with the courage to turn.

CHAPTER 10 — THE STRUCTURE OF DISCUSSION

Discussion is not the softer version of debate.
It is a different structure entirely.

Where debate is adversarial, discussion is cooperative.

Where debate divides people into sides, discussion places them on the same side of the table.

Where debate seeks victory, discussion seeks clarity.

Discussion is built on three movements:

1. Shared intention

2. Shared attention

3. Shared reality

These movements are simple, but they are not easy.

They require a posture of mind that debate never asks for.

1. Shared intention

Discussion begins with a question, not a position.

It begins with the desire to understand, not the desire to win.

This intention shapes everything that follows.

When two people share the intention to understand, the conversation changes direction.

It stops moving toward conflict and begins moving toward clarity.

2. Shared attention

Discussion requires attention that is not split between listening and preparing a response.

It requires attention that is not defensive, strategic, or performative.

Shared attention means both people are looking at the same thing — the question, the idea, the truth — rather than at each other as opponents.

This shift is subtle but transformative.
It turns communication from a battle into a collaboration.

3. Shared reality

Discussion seeks to uncover what is actually true, not what is convenient, familiar, or emotionally satisfying.

Shared reality is not agreement for the sake of harmony.
It is the willingness to examine the world as it is, even when it challenges our assumptions.

In discussion, truth is not something to defend.
It is something to discover.

Discussion is not a technique.
It is a structure — a structure aligned with truth, clarity, and understanding.

Where debate accelerates noise, discussion restores coherence.
Where debate collapses clarity, discussion rebuilds it.
Where debate feeds the ego, discussion frees the mind.

This is the architecture that makes understanding possible.

CHAPTER 11 — THE POSTURE OF LISTENING

Listening is not the act of waiting for your turn to speak.

It is the act of making space for truth to appear.

Most people believe they are listening when they are silent.

But silence is not listening.

Silence can be strategic, defensive, or impatient.

Listening is something else entirely.

Listening is a posture — a way of holding the mind.

It requires stillness, not passivity.

Attention, not agreement.

Openness, not surrender.

Listening is the willingness to let reality speak before the ego does.

In debate, listening is impossible because the mind is occupied.

It is busy preparing responses, defending positions, and scanning for weaknesses.

It is not available to receive anything new.

In discussion, listening becomes the foundation.

It becomes the method.

It becomes the way truth enters the conversation.

The posture of listening has three qualities:

1. Curiosity

2. Humility

3. Presence

1. Curiosity

Curiosity is the desire to see what is actually there, not what we expect to find.

It is the willingness to be surprised.

Curiosity turns the mind outward, toward reality, rather than inward, toward defense.

2. Humility

Humility is not self-doubt.
It is the recognition that our perspective is limited.
Humility makes room for truth to expand beyond our assumptions.
It allows us to revise, refine, and grow.

3. Presence

Presence is the ability to stay with what is happening now.
Not with the argument we rehearsed.
Not with the fear of being wrong.
Not with the desire to win.

Presence is the mind unclenched.

When these three qualities come together, listening becomes transformative.
It becomes the doorway through which clarity enters.
It becomes the method by which understanding becomes possible.

Listening is not weakness.
It is strength.
It is the strength to let truth matter more than victory.

And without this posture, no alternative to debate can succeed.

CHAPTER 12 — THE ART OF ASKING

Questions shape the direction of a conversation.
They determine whether we move toward clarity or toward conflict.
They reveal whether we are seeking truth or seeking advantage.

In debate, questions are weapons.
They are used to trap, expose, or destabilize.
They are designed to win.

In discussion, questions are tools.
They are used to explore, illuminate, and understand.
They are designed to reveal.

The art of asking is the art of opening space — space for truth to emerge, space for assumptions to be examined, space for understanding to grow.

There are three kinds of questions that make discussion possible:

1. Clarifying questions

2. Exploratory questions

3. Reality-anchoring questions

1. Clarifying questions

These questions remove ambiguity.
They ensure that both people are speaking about the same thing.
They prevent confusion before it begins.

Clarifying questions sound simple, but they are powerful:

"What do you mean by that?"

"Can you give an example?"

"Are we talking about the same thing?"

Clarity begins with precision.

2. Exploratory questions

These questions open the landscape.
They invite depth, nuance, and reflection.
They help uncover the structure beneath the surface.

Exploratory questions do not challenge — they illuminate:
"What led you to that conclusion?"
"What are you seeing that I might be missing?"
"What else could be true here?"

Exploration replaces confrontation.

3. Reality-anchoring questions

These questions bring the conversation back to what is actually true.
They cut through assumptions, stories, and emotional momentum.

Reality-anchoring questions restore orientation:
"What evidence do we have?"
"What is the actual situation?"
"What do we know for certain?"

These questions prevent the conversation from drifting into noise.

The art of asking is not about cleverness.
It is about sincerity.
It is about the willingness to see clearly rather than to win quickly.

Questions are not interruptions.
They are invitations — invitations to truth, to clarity, to understanding.

When we ask well, the conversation becomes a shared journey rather than a private performance.

And in that shared journey, truth has room to appear.

CHAPTER 13 — THE SHARED OBJECT

Every meaningful conversation has one requirement:

both people must be looking at the same thing.

This "thing" is the **shared object** — the idea, question, or reality that the conversation is actually about.

Without a shared object, communication collapses into noise.

Debate hides the object.

Discussion reveals it.

In debate, the focus is on the opponent.

The energy is directed sideways — toward defending, attacking, and performing.

The object disappears behind the ego.

In discussion, the focus shifts forward.

Both people turn toward the same point in reality.

The object becomes the anchor.

When the object is shared, the conversation becomes collaborative.

It becomes a joint investigation rather than a private performance.

It becomes a search for truth rather than a struggle for dominance.

The shared object does three things:

1. It stabilizes the conversation

2. It reduces ego involvement

3. It aligns both minds with reality

1. It stabilizes the conversation

When both people are looking at the same object, the conversation stops drifting.

It stops reacting to emotion, tone, or misunderstanding.

It stays grounded.

2. It reduces ego involvement

The moment the object becomes the focus, the opponent stops being the target.

The ego has nothing to defend.

The conversation becomes about the truth, not the self.

3. It aligns both minds with reality

A shared object forces clarity.

It forces precision.

It forces both people to examine what is actually there, not what they assume or fear.

The shared object is the foundation of understanding.

Without it, even the most sincere conversation will collapse into confusion.

With it, even difficult conversations become possible.

The shared object is not a technique.

It is a posture — a way of orienting the mind toward truth rather than victory.

And once two people are looking at the same thing, the possibility of understanding returns.

CHAPTER 14 — THE SLOWING OF PACE

Understanding requires time.

Not much time — just more than debate allows.

Debate accelerates everything.

It pushes the mind into speed, reaction, and performance.

It rewards the quickest answer, not the truest one.

It forces clarity to collapse under the weight of urgency.

Discussion moves differently.

It slows the pace.

It creates space.

It allows the mind to breathe.

Slowing the pace is not hesitation.

It is precision.

It is the refusal to let urgency replace understanding.

It is the recognition that truth does not appear on command.

When the pace slows, several things become possible:

1. The mind can actually think

2. The ego loses its grip

3. The object becomes clearer

4. The conversation becomes human again

1. The mind can actually think

Thought requires time.

Not endless time — just enough time to see what is actually there.

When the pace slows, the mind stops reacting and starts perceiving.

2. The ego loses its grip

The ego thrives on speed.
It needs momentum to stay in control.
When the pace slows, the ego cannot maintain its performance.
It softens.
It loosens.
It lets truth in.

3. The object becomes clearer

When we are not rushing to respond, the shared object comes into focus.
We see details we missed.
We notice assumptions we carried.
We recognize what is real.

4. The conversation becomes human again

Speed dehumanizes.
It turns people into opponents and ideas into weapons.
Slowing the pace restores humanity.
It restores presence.
It restores connection.

The slowing of pace is not a technique.
It is a discipline — a refusal to let urgency dictate truth.
It is the moment the conversation shifts from performance to understanding.

And without this slowing, no alternative to debate can survive.

CHAPTER 15 — THE RETURN TO REALITY

Every conversation drifts.

It drifts into assumptions, emotions, stories, and fears.

It drifts into what we think is happening rather than what is actually happening.

Debate accelerates this drift.

It pushes people away from reality and into performance.

It rewards confidence even when confidence is misplaced.

It rewards certainty even when certainty is false.

Discussion reverses the drift.

It brings the conversation back to reality — the shared, observable, undeniable ground beneath both people.

Reality is the anchor.

Reality is the stabilizer.

Reality is the only place where clarity can survive.

The return to reality requires three movements:

1. Naming what is actually happening

2. Distinguishing fact from interpretation

3. Re-anchoring the conversation in what is real

1. Naming what is actually happening

Most confusion comes from unspoken assumptions.

When we name what is happening — clearly, simply, without accusation — the fog begins to lift.

"This is what I'm seeing."

"This is what I understand so far."

"This is the part that's unclear."

Naming restores orientation.

2. Distinguishing fact from interpretation

Facts are stable.

Interpretations are not.

Debate collapses the two into one.

Discussion separates them.

"What do we know?"

"What are we assuming?"

"What are we adding that might not be there?"

This separation is the beginning of clarity.

3. Re-anchoring the conversation in what is real

When both people return to the same ground, the conversation becomes coherent again.

The shared object becomes visible.

The pace slows.

The ego softens.

The truth becomes accessible.

Reality is not an opinion.

It is not a performance.

It is not a position to defend.

Reality is the place where understanding becomes possible.

The return to reality is not a technique.

It is a discipline — a commitment to truth over narrative, clarity over comfort, and understanding over victory.

Without this return, even the best intentions collapse into noise.

With it, even difficult conversations become navigable.

CHAPTER 16 — THE SHIFT FROM IDENTITY TO TRUTH

Every conversation carries two forces:
the force of identity and the force of truth.

Identity asks, *"What does this say about me?"*
Truth asks, *"What is actually real?"*

Debate strengthens identity.
It turns every idea into a reflection of the self.
It makes being wrong feel like being diminished.
It makes being challenged feel like being attacked.

When identity is at the center, truth becomes secondary.

Discussion reverses this order.
It shifts the center of gravity from identity to truth.
It allows the self to loosen its grip so reality can come into view.

This shift is subtle but transformative.

It begins with a simple recognition:
My identity is not at stake here.

Once identity steps aside, several things become possible:

1. Ideas can be examined without fear
2. Mistakes become information, not threats
3. Questions become invitations, not attacks
4. Truth becomes accessible

1. Ideas can be examined without fear

When identity is not fused with an idea, the idea becomes movable.
It can be explored, questioned, refined, or replaced.
It becomes something we hold, not something that holds us.

2. Mistakes become information, not threats

Being wrong is no longer a humiliation.
It is simply a moment of correction — a step

toward clarity.

Mistakes stop being personal and start being useful.

3. Questions become invitations, not attacks

When identity is not under threat, questions lose their sting.

They become tools for understanding rather than weapons for dominance.

4. Truth becomes accessible

Truth does not compete with identity.

It simply waits for space.

When identity loosens, truth appears.

The shift from identity to truth is not a technique.

It is a reorientation — a turning of the mind toward what is real rather than what is protective.

This shift is the foundation of all meaningful communication.

Without it, even the best methods collapse.

With it, even difficult conversations become possible.

Understanding begins when identity steps aside and truth steps forward.

CHAPTER 17 — THE EMERGENCE OF CLARITY

Clarity does not appear all at once.
It emerges.

It emerges when the noise settles.
It emerges when the ego loosens.
It emerges when the pace slows enough for reality
to come into focus.

Clarity is not something we create.
It is something we uncover.

It has been there the entire time — beneath the
assumptions, beneath the reactions, beneath the
performance.
Clarity is what remains when everything
unnecessary falls away.

The emergence of clarity follows a pattern:
1. The object becomes visible
2. The mind becomes still
3. The truth becomes simple

1. The object becomes visible

Once both people are looking at the same thing,
the conversation stabilizes.
The fog lifts.
The confusion dissolves.
The object stands in the open, no longer distorted
by fear or urgency.

2. The mind becomes still

Stillness is not silence.
It is the absence of internal conflict.
It is the moment when the mind stops defending
and starts perceiving.
Stillness allows truth to be seen without distortion.

3. The truth becomes simple

Truth is rarely complicated.
It is usually direct, grounded, and obvious once
seen.
The complexity comes from the noise surrounding
it — the stories, the fears, the identities, the
assumptions.

When clarity emerges, the complexity collapses.
What once felt tangled becomes straightforward.
What once felt overwhelming becomes
manageable.
What once felt impossible becomes clear.

Clarity is not a reward.
It is a consequence — the natural outcome of a
conversation aligned with reality rather than ego.

It cannot be forced.
It cannot be rushed.
It cannot be performed.

But when the conditions are right — when the
pace slows, when the object is shared, when
identity steps aside — clarity emerges on its own.

And once clarity appears, everything changes.

CHAPTER 18 — THE CONDITIONS FOR UNDERSTANDING

Understanding is not mysterious.

It is not unpredictable.

It is not something that appears at random.

Understanding arises when the right conditions are present — just as clarity emerges when noise subsides, and truth appears when identity loosens.

These conditions are simple, but they are not common.

They require a different posture of mind, a different structure of communication, and a different relationship to truth.

There are four conditions that make understanding possible:

1. A shared object

2. A slowed pace

3. A softened ego

4. A return to reality

1. A shared object

Both people must be looking at the same thing.

Not at each other.

Not at their own assumptions.

Not at their fears or interpretations.

The shared object anchors the conversation.

It stabilizes the mind.

It creates the possibility of clarity.

2. A slowed pace

Understanding cannot survive urgency.

It requires time — not much, just enough for the mind to see rather than react.

When the pace slows, the ego loses momentum.

The mind becomes available.

Truth becomes visible.

3. A softened ego

The ego is not the enemy.
It is simply too loud.

When the ego softens — when identity is no longer at stake — ideas become movable.
Questions become safe.
Mistakes become information.

A softened ego creates the space where truth can enter.

4. A return to reality

Reality is the ground beneath both people.
It is the stabilizer.
It is the reference point that prevents the conversation from drifting into stories, assumptions, and performances.

When both minds return to what is actually happening, understanding becomes possible again.

Understanding is not a technique.
It is a phenomenon — the natural outcome of a conversation aligned with truth rather than ego, with reality rather than reaction.

When these conditions are present, understanding emerges on its own.
When they are absent, no amount of intelligence or goodwill can compensate.

Understanding is not something we force.
It is something we allow.

PART IV — THE METHOD

Understanding is not an accident.
It is the result of a structure — a way of moving, seeing, and speaking that aligns the mind with reality rather than ego.

This part of the book reveals that structure.

It gathers everything from the previous movements — the collapse of debate, the emergence of discussion, the conditions for clarity — and turns them into a method that anyone can use.

This is not a script.
It is not a set of tricks.
It is not a list of techniques to memorize.

It is a way of orienting the mind.

A way of approaching conversations that makes understanding possible, even in difficult moments.
A way of restoring clarity where confusion once dominated.
A way of thinking together rather than fighting alone.

CHAPTER 19 — THE OBJECT

Every method begins with a first move.

In communication, the first move determines the direction of the entire conversation.

Debate begins with a position.

Discussion begins with a question.

This difference is everything.

A position divides.

A question opens.

A position demands defense.

A question invites exploration.

A position triggers the ego.

A question awakens the mind.

The first move of discussion is simple:

Name the object.

Not your opinion.

Not your conclusion.

Not your argument.

The object.

"What exactly are we talking about?"

"What is the question we're trying to answer?"

"What is the thing we're both looking at?"

This move does three things at once:

1. It stabilizes the conversation

2. It slows the pace

3. It softens the ego

1. It stabilizes the conversation

Most confusion begins before the conversation even starts — when two people think they are talking about the same thing but are actually talking about different things.

Naming the object prevents this drift.

It creates a shared anchor.

2. It slows the pace

The moment the object is named, urgency dissolves.
The conversation stops accelerating toward conflict and begins moving toward clarity.

3. It softens the ego

When the object becomes the focus, the self is no longer the center.
The ego has nothing to defend.
The conversation becomes about truth, not identity.

The first move is not dramatic.
It is not clever.
It is not confrontational.

It is simply the act of orienting both minds toward the same point in reality.

Once the object is named, the conversation can begin.
Without this move, the conversation never truly starts.

CHAPTER 20 — THE PACE

Once the object is named, the conversation has a direction.

But direction is not enough.

The mind must settle.

The noise must fall away.

The ego must loosen its grip.

The second move of the method is simple:

Slow the pace.

Not dramatically.

Not theatrically.

Just enough to let the mind shift from reaction to perception.

Debate accelerates.

Discussion decelerates.

This slowing is not hesitation.

It is not weakness.

It is not uncertainty.

It is the deliberate creation of space — space for clarity, space for thought, space for truth.

The second move does three things:

1. It interrupts the ego's momentum

2. It restores cognitive availability

3. It prepares the mind for understanding

1. It interrupts the ego's momentum

The ego thrives on speed.

It needs urgency to maintain control.

When the pace slows, the ego cannot keep performing.

Its grip weakens.

Its defensiveness softens.

2. It restores cognitive availability

A fast mind is a reactive mind.

A slowed mind is a perceptive mind.

When the pace slows, attention becomes available again.
The mind can actually think rather than defend.
It can see rather than assume.

3. It prepares the mind for understanding

Understanding requires stillness.
Not silence — stillness.
A mind that is not rushing, not rehearsing, not preparing its next move.

Slowing the pace creates the conditions for clarity to emerge.

The second move is not a technique.
It is a discipline — a refusal to let urgency dictate truth.

It is the moment the conversation shifts from reaction to reflection.
From performance to presence.
From noise to clarity.

Once the pace slows, the conversation becomes capable of understanding.

CHAPTER 21 — CLARIYING MEANING

Once the object is named and the pace has slowed, the conversation becomes stable enough for the third move:

Clarify what is actually being said.

Not what you think the other person means.

Not what you fear they mean.

Not what you are preparing to respond to.

What they are actually saying.

This move is simple:

Ask a clarifying question.

Not to challenge.

Not to trap.

Not to expose a flaw.

To understand.

Clarifying questions are the backbone of discussion.

They prevent drift.

They dissolve assumptions.

They reveal the structure beneath the words.

The third move does three things:

1. It aligns both minds with the same meaning

2. It prevents unnecessary conflict

3. It deepens the shared object

1. It aligns both minds with the same meaning

Most conflict begins with misinterpretation.

A single word can carry different meanings for different people.

A clarifying question brings both minds into alignment.

"What do you mean by that?"

"Can you say that another way?"

"Is this the right interpretation?"

Alignment replaces assumption.

2. It prevents unnecessary conflict

When meaning is unclear, the ego fills the gap with fear, projection, or defensiveness.

Clarification removes the ambiguity that fuels conflict.

It is easier to understand someone than to fight a misunderstanding.

3. It deepens the shared object

Every clarifying question sharpens the object.

It becomes more precise, more visible, more grounded in reality.

The conversation becomes more stable with each refinement.

The third move is not interrogation.

It is not skepticism.

It is not doubt.

It is care.

It is the willingness to understand before responding.

It is the discipline of refusing to build on assumptions.

Once meaning is clarified, the conversation becomes capable of depth.

Without this move, the conversation collapses into confusion.

CHAPTER 22 — RETURNING TO REALITY

Once the object is named, the pace is slowed, and the meaning is clarified, the conversation is finally stable enough for the fourth move:

Return to reality.

Not to emotion.

Not to assumption.

Not to interpretation.

Reality.

This move is the anchor of the entire method. It is the moment where the conversation reconnects with what is actually happening rather than what each person imagines is happening.

The fourth move is simple:

Distinguish what is known from what is assumed.

This distinction is the foundation of clarity.

"What do we actually know?"

"What is the evidence?"

"What is the real situation?"

"What are we adding that might not be there?"

These questions do not challenge the person. They challenge the drift.

The fourth move does three things:

1. It dissolves confusion

2. It stabilizes the shared object

3. It restores orientation

1. It dissolves confusion

Most confusion comes from mixing facts with interpretations.

When the two are separated, the fog lifts.

The conversation becomes clear again.

2. It stabilizes the shared object

Reality is the most stable reference point available.

When both people return to it, the object becomes sharper, more grounded, more precise.

3. It restores orientation

Reality is the compass.

It prevents drift.

It prevents escalation.

It prevents the conversation from collapsing into stories and fears.

The fourth move is not confrontation.

It is not skepticism.

It is not doubt.

It is orientation — the act of returning both minds to the same ground.

Without this move, the conversation floats. With it, the conversation becomes anchored, coherent, and capable of truth.

The return to reality is the moment the method becomes real.

CHAPTER 23 — INVITING TRUTH

Once the object is shared, the pace is slowed, the meaning is clarified, and the conversation has returned to reality, the method reaches its most powerful moment:

Ask the question that reveals the truth.

Not a question that challenges.

Not a question that traps.

Not a question that performs intelligence.

A question that opens.

A question that brings the truth into view for both people at once.

This is the fifth move:

Invite the other person to look at the object with you.

Not at you.

Not at themselves.

At the object.

"What do you see when you look at this?"

"What seems true to you here?"

"What part of this feels most important?"

"What do you think is actually happening?"

These questions do not push.

They reveal.

The fifth move does three things:

1. It turns the conversation into a shared investigation
2. It dissolves the last remnants of ego
3. It allows truth to emerge naturally

The conversation becomes a shared investigation

The moment both people are looking at the same object and asking the same question, the conversation becomes collaborative.

It becomes a joint search rather than a private defense.

The ego dissolves

When the question is about the object, not the person, the ego has nothing to protect.

It cannot perform.

It cannot defend.

It can only observe.

Truth emerges naturally

Truth does not need to be forced.

It needs to be seen.

When both minds are oriented toward the same object, at the same pace, with the same clarity, truth becomes visible without effort.

The fifth move is not persuasion.

It is not argument.

It is not strategy.

It is invitation — the invitation to see what is real.

Once this move is made, the conversation becomes capable of understanding.

It becomes capable of resolution.

It becomes capable of truth.

CHAPTER 24 — THE SHIFT

Every method has a moment where everything turns.

A moment where the conversation crosses from exploration into understanding.

A moment where the mind stops defending and starts seeing.

This moment is not dramatic.

It is not loud.

It is not a breakthrough in the way people imagine breakthroughs.

It is a shift.

A subtle, internal reorientation —

from resistance to openness,

from tension to ease,

from confusion to clarity.

The shift is not something you force.

It is something you allow.

It happens when the conditions are right:

- The object is clear
- The pace is slow
- The meaning is understood
- Reality is shared
- Truth has been invited

When these movements align, the mind enters a different posture.

It becomes receptive.

It becomes available.

It becomes capable of understanding.

The shift is the moment the conversation stops being about winning or protecting or performing

—

and becomes about seeing.

Seeing what is real.

Seeing what is true.

Seeing what has been there the entire time.

This shift is the heart of the method.

It is the point where understanding becomes possible.

It is the moment the conversation transforms.

You cannot manufacture the shift.

You cannot demand it.

You cannot rush it.

You can only create the conditions in which it naturally appears.

And when it appears, everything changes.

The conversation becomes human again.

The mind becomes clear again.

Truth becomes visible again.

The shift is not the end of the method.

It is the beginning of understanding.

PART V — LIVING THE METHOD

A method is only alive when it is lived.

It is one thing to understand the structure —
the object, the pace, the meaning, the return to
reality, the invitation to truth, the shift.

It is another thing to carry this structure into
real conversations, real tensions, real relationships,
real moments where clarity is needed and ego is
loud.

This part of the book is about embodiment.

Not theory.

Not technique.

Not performance.

Embodiment.

How the method feels in practice.

How it moves in real time.

How it changes the posture of the mind.

How it transforms the way we speak, listen, and
understand.

This section is not about adding more steps.
It is about showing how the method becomes a
way of being —
a way of approaching conversations that restores
clarity, preserves humanity, and makes
understanding possible even in difficult moments.

Part V is where the method becomes lived
reality.

CHAPTER 25 — THE POSTURE

A method is only as strong as the posture that carries it.

You can know the movements —

the object, the pace, the meaning, the return to reality, the invitation to truth, the shift —

and still lose the conversation if your posture collapses.

Posture is not physical.

It is internal.

It is the way the mind holds itself while speaking and listening.

Posture determines whether the method lives or dies in practice.

There are three elements to the posture:

1. Openness

2. Presence

3. Orientation

Openness

Openness is the willingness to see what is real, even if it disrupts what you believe.

It is the refusal to defend prematurely.

It is the recognition that truth is not threatened by investigation.

Openness is not vulnerability.

It is strength — the strength to let reality speak.

Presence

Presence is the ability to stay with the moment rather than with your rehearsed responses.

It is the discipline of listening without preparing your next move.

It is the quieting of the internal noise that distorts understanding.

Presence is not passivity.

It is attention.

Orientation

Orientation is the direction of the mind.

It is the commitment to look at the object rather than at yourself.

It is the choice to anchor the conversation in reality rather than in identity.

Orientation is not neutrality.

It is clarity.

Posture is the invisible architecture beneath the method.

It is what allows the movements to work.

Without posture, the method becomes mechanical.

With posture, the method becomes alive.

The posture is the difference between performing the method and embodying it.

When the posture is right, the method becomes natural.

Effortless.

Human.

This is how the method enters the world — not as a technique, but as a way of being.

CHAPTER 26 — THE FEELING OF CLARITY

Clarity is not an idea.

It is a feeling.

A quiet one.

A steady one.

A feeling that arrives not with force, but with relief.

Most people think clarity is a moment of brilliance — a flash of insight, a sudden revelation, a dramatic breakthrough.

But clarity is rarely loud.

It is rarely explosive.

It is rarely cinematic.

Clarity feels like **something settling**.

It feels like the mind exhaling.

It feels like tension dissolving.

It feels like the noise inside you finally stepping aside.

Clarity is the moment when the conversation stops pulling you in different directions and begins to align.

It is the moment when the object becomes visible.

It is the moment when the truth stops hiding.

Clarity feels like:

- **ease** instead of strain
- **space** instead of pressure
- **orientation** instead of confusion
- **lightness** instead of heaviness
- **stillness** instead of urgency

Clarity is not the end of the conversation.

It is the beginning of understanding.

When clarity appears, the ego softens.

The mind opens.

The posture stabilizes.
The conversation becomes human again.

Clarity is not something you create.
It is something you uncover.

It emerges when the noise falls away —
when the object is clear,
when the pace is slow,
when meaning is understood,
when reality is shared,
when truth is invited,
when the shift has occurred.

Clarity is the natural state of a mind that is no longer fighting itself.

This is why the method works.
Not because it teaches you what to say,
but because it restores the conditions in which clarity can be felt.

And once clarity is felt, understanding becomes possible

CHAPTER 27 — WHEN THE METHOD FAILS

No method works everywhere.

Not because the method is weak,

but because some conditions make understanding impossible.

The method does not fail because you used it incorrectly.

It fails because the environment does not allow clarity to survive.

There are three situations where the method cannot function:

1. When the other person refuses reality

2. When the ego is fully activated

3. When the conversation is not actually a conversation

1. When the other person refuses reality

If someone is committed to a story, a fantasy, or a narrative that protects their identity, the method cannot reach them.

You can return to reality, but they will not follow.

You can clarify meaning, but they will distort it.

You can invite truth, but they will decline the invitation.

The method requires at least a minimal willingness to see what is real.

Without that willingness, the conversation is not about truth —

it is about protection.

2. When the ego is fully activated

A fully activated ego cannot listen.

It cannot see.

It cannot receive.

It is not a mind — it is a shield.

When the ego is in full defense mode, the method cannot land.

The pace will not slow.

The object will not stabilize.

Meaning will not clarify.

The ego must soften before the method can work.

Sometimes that softening takes minutes.

Sometimes it takes years.

Sometimes it never comes.

3. When the conversation is not actually a conversation

Some interactions are not conversations at all.

They are performances.

They are monologues.

They are emotional releases.

They are battles disguised as dialogue.

The method cannot function in a space where there is no shared intention to understand.

A conversation requires two minds.

A performance requires only one.

The method does not fail because you failed.

It fails because the conditions for understanding are absent.

And this is not a flaw.

It is a boundary.

A method without boundaries is not a method

—

it is a fantasy.

Understanding requires:

- a shared object
- a slowed pace

- clarified meaning
- a return to reality
- an invitation to truth
- a willingness to shift

If any of these are impossible, the method cannot function.

This chapter is not a warning.

It is a protection.

It protects you from taking responsibility for what is not yours.

It protects the method from being misused.

It protects the conversation from becoming a battlefield.

The method works —

but only where understanding is possible.

CHAPTER 28 — THE COST OF CLARITY

Clarity is a gift, but it is not without a price.

Most people want clarity until they realize what it demands.

They want truth until they see what truth requires them to release.

They want understanding until they feel what understanding asks them to confront.

Clarity is not comfortable.

It is not gentle.

It is not painless.

Clarity costs something.

It costs the stories you've been telling yourself.

It costs the illusions you've been protecting.

It costs the identities you've been defending.

It costs the narratives that kept you safe but kept you blind.

Clarity asks you to let go of:

- the need to be right
- the need to win
- the need to protect your image
- the need to control the outcome
- the need to preserve your old self

Clarity is not just seeing what is true.

It is accepting what is true.

And acceptance is the cost.

The moment clarity arrives, something inside you shifts —

and something inside you must be surrendered.

Sometimes what you surrender is small:

a misunderstanding, a false assumption, a misplaced fear.

Sometimes what you surrender is large:
a belief you've held for years,
a story you've built your identity around,
a way of seeing the world that no longer fits reality.
    Clarity is not cruel.
But it is honest.
    It does not negotiate with illusions.
It does not compromise with ego.
It does not soften the truth to protect your feelings.
    Clarity reveals what is real —
and asks you to live in alignment with it.
    This is the cost.
    And yet, the cost is worth it.
    Because on the other side of clarity is freedom.
On the other side of clarity is peace.
On the other side of clarity is a life that is no longer
built on confusion, fear, or distortion.
    Clarity costs something —
but confusion costs more.

CHAPTER 29 — THE RETURN TO HUMANITY

Understanding is not just an intellectual achievement.

It is a human one.

The method is not merely a structure for clarity.

It is a way of returning to the person in front of you —

not as an opponent,

not as a threat,

not as a problem to solve,

but as a human being.

Debate dehumanizes.

It turns people into positions.

It turns conversations into battles.

It turns minds into weapons.

The method reverses this.

It restores the human element that debate erases.

When the object is clear,

when the pace is slow,

when meaning is understood,

when reality is shared,

when truth is invited,

when the shift occurs —

something else happens beneath the surface.

You begin to see the other person again.

Not their argument.

Not their defensiveness.

Not their performance.

Them.

Their fear.

Their confusion.

Their sincerity.

Their longing to be understood.
Their desire to be seen.
Their humanity.
The return to humanity is not sentimental.
It is not emotional.
It is not dramatic.
It is simple.
It is the recognition that the person you are
speaking with is not your enemy.
They are another mind trying to navigate reality,
just like you.
This recognition changes everything.
It softens the tone.
It opens the posture.
It dissolves the tension.
It makes space for compassion without sacrificing
clarity.
Humanity does not replace truth.
It makes truth bearable.
Humanity does not weaken the method.
It strengthens it.
Because understanding is not just about seeing
what is real —
it is about seeing who is real.
The return to humanity is the moment the
conversation becomes whole again.
It is the moment the method becomes more than a
structure.
It becomes a way of relating.
A way of being with others that honors both
truth and personhood.
This is the heart of the method.
Not clarity alone.

Not truth alone.
Not structure alone.
Humanity.

CHAPTER 30 — THE GIFT OF UNDERSTANDING

Understanding is not an achievement.
It is a gift.

Not a gift you give to someone else,
but a gift you give to the space between you —
the space where truth can live.

Understanding is the moment when two minds,
after moving through confusion, ego, fear, and
noise,
finally meet in the same reality.

It is not victory.
It is not defeat.
It is not compromise.

It is recognition.

Recognition of what is real.
Recognition of what is true.
Recognition of the humanity in the other person.
Recognition of the humanity in yourself.

Understanding is not agreement.
Agreement is optional.
Understanding is essential.

You can understand someone without adopting
their view.
You can understand someone without surrendering
your own.
You can understand someone without collapsing
into their world.

Understanding is the bridge —
the connection that makes clarity possible
without requiring sameness.

The gift of understanding is threefold:

- **It restores peace**
- **It restores connection**

- **It restores truth**

It restores peace

When understanding appears, the internal tension dissolves.
The mind stops fighting.
The ego stops performing.
The conversation stops spiraling.
Peace returns because the noise has fallen away.

It restores connection

Understanding is the moment you see the other person again —
not as an opponent,
not as a threat,
not as a position,
but as a human being.
Connection returns because the walls have lowered.

It restores truth

Truth is not something you impose.
Truth is something you uncover together.
Understanding is the moment truth becomes visible to both minds at once.
Understanding is not rare.
It is simply buried beneath layers of fear, ego, urgency, and confusion.
The method does not create understanding.
It reveals it.
It clears the space.
It slows the pace.
It aligns the meaning.
It returns to reality.
It invites truth.
It allows the shift.

And when the shift happens,
understanding emerges like something that was
waiting for you the entire time.
This is the gift.
Not clarity alone.
Not truth alone.
Not technique alone.
Understanding.
The quiet, steady, human recognition
that makes communication possible
and makes life bearable.

CHAPTER 31 — THE END OF DEBATE

Debate ends where understanding begins.

Debate is not a search for truth.

It is a search for victory.

It is a performance of intelligence, not an encounter with reality.

It is a battle of egos, not a meeting of minds.

Debate destroys clarity.

It distorts meaning.

It accelerates pace.

It replaces reality with narrative.

It rewards the loudest voice, not the truest one.

Debate is not conversation.

It is combat.

And combat has no interest in truth.

The method ends debate because it removes the fuel that debate feeds on:

- confusion
- speed
- ego
- misinterpretation
- narrative
- identity

When the object is clear, debate has nothing to attack.

When the pace is slow, debate has nothing to escalate.

When meaning is clarified, debate has nothing to distort.

When reality is shared, debate has nothing to deny.

When truth is invited, debate has nothing to defend.

When the shift occurs, debate has nothing left to stand on.

Debate collapses because the conditions that
sustain it no longer exist.

The method does not defeat debate.
It dissolves it.

It replaces combat with clarity.
It replaces performance with presence.
It replaces ego with orientation.
It replaces noise with understanding.

Debate ends not because one person wins,
but because both people return to reality.

And in reality, there is nothing to fight.

There is only what is true.

The end of debate is not silence.
It is not surrender.
It is not agreement.

It is the moment when the conversation
becomes human again —
when truth becomes visible,
when clarity becomes possible,
when understanding becomes the shared goal.

Debate ends where humanity returns.

This is the purpose of the method.
Not to win arguments.
Not to dominate conversations.
Not to outthink another mind.

The purpose is to restore the conditions in
which truth can be seen
and people can meet each other again
without the armor of ego
or the weapons of debate.

The end of debate is the beginning of
understanding.

CHAPTER 32 — THE METHOD IN THE WORLD

A method is only proven when it meets the world.

Not the ideal world.
Not the theoretical world.
The real one —
the world of misunderstandings,
interruptions,
defensiveness,
emotion,
fear,
and noise.

The world where conversations rarely unfold cleanly.
The world where people speak from pain, not clarity.
The world where truth is often buried beneath layers of urgency and identity.

This is where the method must live.

The method is not designed for perfect conditions.
It is designed for human conditions.

It works in:

- relationships
- friendships
- workplaces
- conflicts
- misunderstandings
- moments of tension
- moments of confusion
- moments where clarity feels impossible

The method does not require the world to be calm.

It creates calm.
It does not require the world to be clear.
It creates clarity.
It does not require the world to be slow.
It slows the world down.

The method is not fragile.
It is resilient.

It can withstand emotion.
It can withstand confusion.
It can withstand ego — up to a point.
It can withstand the chaos of real human interaction.

Because the method is not about control.
It is about orientation.

It gives you a way to move through conversations without being pulled into the spiral of reaction.
It gives you a way to stay grounded when the other person is not.
It gives you a way to return to reality even when the conversation is drifting away from it.

The method in the world looks like:

- naming the object when things get blurry
- slowing the pace when things get heated
- clarifying meaning when things get tangled
- returning to reality when things get distorted
- inviting truth when things get defensive
- allowing the shift when things finally soften

The method is not something you impose.
It is something you embody.

And when you embody it, the world responds.

Not always immediately.
Not always predictably.
Not always gently.
But eventually, the world recognizes clarity.
It recognizes steadiness.
It recognizes truth.
The method in the world is not about changing
others.
It is about changing the conditions in which
understanding becomes possible.
And when the conditions change,
the conversation changes.
The relationship changes.
The outcome changes.
The world changes.
Not all at once.
Not dramatically.
But steadily —
one conversation at a time.

CHAPTER 33 — THE LIMITS OF LANGUAGE

Language is powerful, but it is not infinite.

It can name the object.

It can slow the pace.

It can clarify meaning.

It can return the conversation to reality.

It can invite truth.

It can guide the shift.

But language cannot do everything.

There are moments when words reach their limit —

not because the truth is too complex,

but because the truth is too simple.

Language struggles with simplicity.

It struggles with silence.

It struggles with presence.

It struggles with the parts of reality that cannot be divided into sentences.

There are truths that can be spoken,

and there are truths that can only be seen.

There are understandings that can be explained,

and there are understandings that can only be felt.

There are moments in conversation where the method has done its work,

clarity has emerged,

understanding is present,

and yet words would only get in the way.

This is the limit of language.

The limit is not a failure.

It is a threshold.

A threshold where the conversation moves from speaking to seeing,

from explaining to recognizing,
from describing to understanding.

Language can bring two minds to the edge of
truth,
but it cannot cross the threshold for them.

The crossing happens in silence —
in presence,
in openness,
in the shared recognition of what is real.

This is why the method is not a linguistic
technique.
It is a way of orienting the mind.

Because once the mind is oriented correctly,
language becomes optional.

The truth becomes visible without being
spoken.
The understanding becomes mutual without being
articulated.
The connection becomes real without being
described.

The limits of language are not the limits of
understanding.
They are simply the point where understanding no
longer needs words.

This is where the method becomes more than
communication.
It becomes communion —
a meeting of minds in the space beyond language.

CHAPTER 34 — THE SILENCE AFTER UNDERSTANDING

Understanding has a sound.
It is not loud.
It is not triumphant.
It is not dramatic.
It is silence.
Not the silence of avoidance,
not the silence of tension,
not the silence of withdrawal.
A different silence —
a silence that feels like the mind finally resting.

The silence after understanding is the moment
when the conversation no longer needs words to
hold itself together.
The truth is present.
The object is clear.
The tension has dissolved.
The ego has softened.
The posture is steady.
There is nothing left to defend.
Nothing left to prove.
Nothing left to untangle.

The silence after understanding is the space
where everything settles.
It feels like:

- a deep exhale
- a loosening in the chest
- a quieting of the internal noise
- a sense of alignment
- a return to yourself

This silence is not empty.
It is full —
full of recognition,

full of clarity,
full of the simple relief of seeing what is real.

The silence after understanding is the moment
the conversation becomes whole.
It is the moment the method completes its work.
It is the moment where presence replaces language.

This silence is not the end of the relationship.
It is the beginning of a new one.

A relationship grounded in clarity rather than
confusion,
in reality rather than narrative,
in understanding rather than debate.

The silence after understanding is the proof that
the method has worked.
Not because the conversation ended,
but because the noise ended.

This silence is the natural conclusion of truth.

CHAPTER 35 — THE RESTORATION

Every conversation that loses its way loses the same thing:

orientation.

Orientation toward the object.

Orientation toward reality.

Orientation toward truth.

Orientation toward each other.

Confusion is not the absence of intelligence.

It is the absence of orientation.

Debate is not the presence of clarity.

It is the presence of ego.

Misunderstanding is not a failure of language.

It is a failure of alignment.

The method exists for one purpose:

to restore what was lost.

Not to win.

Not to dominate.

Not to impress.

Not to perform.

To restore.

To restore clarity where there was confusion.

To restore reality where there was narrative.

To restore meaning where there was distortion.

To restore humanity where there was conflict.

To restore understanding where there was noise.

Restoration is not dramatic.

It is not loud.

It is not triumphant.

It is quiet.

It is steady.

It is human.

Restoration feels like the mind returning to itself.

It feels like the conversation returning to truth.
It feels like two people returning to the same world
after drifting apart.

Restoration is the natural conclusion of the
method because the method is not about control
—

it is about alignment.

Alignment with what is real.
Alignment with what is true.
Alignment with the person in front of you.
Alignment with yourself.

When the object is named,
when the pace is slowed,
when meaning is clarified,
when reality is restored,
when truth is invited,
when the shift occurs,
when understanding emerges,
when silence settles —

what remains is restoration.

The restoration of the conversation.
The restoration of the relationship.
The restoration of the mind.

This is the end of the method.
Not because nothing more can be said,
but because nothing more is needed.

The method returns you to the place where all
real conversations begin:

a shared reality,

a steady posture,

and a clear mind.

This is the restoration.
This is the purpose.
This is the gift.

EPILOGUE — WHEN CLARITY RETURNS

Every conversation is a small version of a larger truth.

When clarity returns between two people,
it returns to the world in miniature.
When understanding appears in one moment,
it becomes possible in many moments.
When truth is seen in a single exchange,
it becomes easier to see everywhere.

This is why the method matters.

Not because it teaches you how to win,
but because it teaches you how to return —
to reality,
to truth,
to each other,
to yourself.

The world is full of noise.
Full of speed.
Full of confusion.
Full of conversations that never touch what is real.

But clarity is never gone.
It is only covered.

Understanding is never lost.
It is only waiting.

Truth is never fragile.
It is only ignored.

The method does not create clarity.
It uncovers it.

It does not create understanding.
It restores it.

It does not create truth.
It reveals it.

And once you have seen how clarity returns,
you cannot unsee it.

You begin to notice the object sooner.
You slow the pace without effort.
You clarify meaning instinctively.
You return to reality without fear.
You invite truth without hesitation.
You feel the shift before it happens.

The method becomes less of a structure
and more of a way of being.

A way of speaking.
A way of listening.
A way of seeing.

A way of living in a world
that desperately needs people
who can hold clarity
without aggression,
truth
without arrogance,
and understanding
without surrendering themselves.

This is the quiet work.
The human work.
The work that changes conversations
and slowly, steadily,
changes lives.

When clarity returns,
so do we.

FINAL AUTHOR'S NOTE

If you have reached this page, you have walked with me through the full arc of this work —
through confusion, clarity, truth, and the quiet restoration that follows understanding.

I did not write this book to teach you how to win arguments.
I wrote it because I have seen what happens when conversations lose their way —
how easily meaning collapses,
how quickly people drift from reality,
how deeply misunderstanding wounds the human spirit.

I wrote this because clarity matters.
Truth matters.
Understanding matters.
And the way we speak to one another shapes the world we live in.

This method is not mine.
It is something I discovered by necessity —
in the ruins of conversations that failed,
in the aftermath of truths that were not heard,
in the quiet moments where understanding finally returned.

What you have read is not a technique.
It is a way of being.
A way of seeing.
A way of holding yourself in the presence of another mind.

If this book has given you anything —
a moment of recognition,
a shift in posture,
a return to reality,

a glimpse of clarity —
then it has done its work.
    Carry it gently.
Use it wisely.
Let it shape the way you listen,
the way you speak,
the way you meet the world.
    And when conversations become tangled,
when meaning blurs,
when truth feels distant,
when the noise grows loud —
remember that clarity is never gone.
It is only waiting to be uncovered.
    Thank you for walking this path with me.
May your conversations be clear,
your posture steady,
and your understanding deep.

— **Conde Cagalitan**

Dedication

For those who have ever felt unheard,
misunderstood,
or lost inside a conversation that never touched
what was real.

For the ones who kept reaching for clarity
even when the world rewarded noise.

For every mind that longed to be seen
without having to fight,
perform,
or defend itself.

This book is for you.

May you find the courage to slow down,
the strength to return to reality,
and the quiet confidence to speak from truth
rather than fear.

And may your conversations —
with others,
with the world,
and with yourself —
become places where understanding can finally live.

If you want, I can now craft:

- **Acknowledgements**
- **Back-cover closing line**
- **A Blessing for the Reader**
- **A Note on the Canon**

Just tell me where you want to move next.

Acknowledgements

A book like this is never written alone.

It is shaped in the quiet hours,
in the difficult conversations,
in the moments where clarity felt distant
and understanding felt impossible.

To those who challenged me,
who questioned me,
who misunderstood me,
and who forced me to refine what I believed —
your resistance sharpened this work more than
agreement ever could.

To those who listened with patience,
who asked honest questions,
who sought truth without fear —
your openness made this method real long before it
was written.

To the friends who held space for my thinking,
who allowed me to test ideas,
who stayed steady when the path was unclear —
your presence made the work possible.

To the readers who carry this book into their
own lives,
into their own relationships,
into their own difficult conversations —
you are the reason this method exists.

And to the quiet moments,
the ones that revealed truth without words,
the ones that restored clarity when I least expected
it —
I am grateful.

This book is the result of many minds,
many conversations,
many thresholds.

Thank you for walking this one with me.

*A clear mind changes every
conversation — and every life it touches.*

A Blessing for the Reader

May clarity find you gently.
May it arrive not as force,
but as a quiet recognition of what has always been
true.

May your conversations become places of
steadiness,
where meaning is not lost,
where truth is not feared,
and where understanding can finally breathe.

May you learn to slow the pace
when the world demands speed,
to return to reality
when confusion pulls you away,
and to speak from the grounded place within you
that does not need to win to be whole.

May you meet others with openness,
yourself with honesty,
and the world with a mind that is clear enough
to see what is real.

And when noise rises,
when tension builds,
when the path becomes tangled —
may you remember that clarity is never gone.
It is only waiting to be uncovered.

Walk with steadiness.
Speak with truth.
Listen with humanity.

You are capable of more understanding
than you have ever been taught to expect.

A Note on the Canon

This book is part of a larger body of work —
a canon built to answer the deepest human
questions
with clarity, precision, and humanity.

Each volume stands alone,
yet each one is a threshold into the next.
Together, they form a single movement:
from confusion to clarity,
from fragmentation to coherence,
from disorientation to truth.

This book focuses on the architecture of
understanding —
how conversations break,
how clarity returns,
and how truth becomes visible again.

Other volumes explore the nature of reality,
the structure of the self,
the foundations of worldview,
and the journey of becoming fully human.

You do not need to read them in order.
You only need to follow the thread of recognition
—
the quiet sense that something true is being
uncovered.

The canon is not a system.
It is a restoration.
A return to what is real,
what is human,
and what has always been true.

If this book opened something in you,
the others will meet you where this one leaves off.

If you want, I can now assemble:

- the **full front matter** in correct publishing order
- the **full back matter**
- or a **ceremonial closing page** to end the book with a single line

Just tell me where you want to go next.